Moonlit Madness

Embracing the Twilight Studio

S. J. Brown

BookLeaf Publishing

India | USA | UK

Made with ❤ on the BookLeaf Publishing Platform
www.bookleafpub.in
www.bookleafpub.com

Dedication

For the early birds who retire by 9pm, awakening after midnight to strange magic and musings -- may we always keep notebooks by our bedsides.

Preface

This collection of poems was inspired by twilight reflections, midnight dreams and nightmares. They are the result of a nightly journey through the witching hour and beyond. The poems reverence the delicate relationship between nature and self, imagination and reality. Each piece reflects fragments of nights spent in contemplation, embracing the vivid dreams and feelings that arise only in tranquil solitude. The "twilight studio" is more than a place or time; it is a space for introspection, an intermediate threshold where one might glimpse the mysteries and epiphanies that linger at the edge of our waking lives.

I hope these poems offer you comfort in the familiar ache of memory and wonder, a safe space to explore strange commonalities in shared experiences. If these words ignite something within you, a flicker of recognition or a lingering echo, then this journey will have found its purpose.

Acknowledgements

My deepest gratitude to everyone who helped breathe life into my art.

My God, thank you for waking me up in the middle of the night to speak to me. Thank you for making space in my beautiful, hectic life for me to deal with the substance of my being.

To my husband, my family, and my closest friends -- thank you for your love, investment, and acceptance. Thank you for reading my work without judgement. Thank you for your honest feedback and companionship. You give me courage to embrace the weird and write it all down. You make me better.

And lastly, to you, dear reader -- thank you for stepping into these moments with me and giving my art a chance. May we embrace our curiosities with our every breath. May we chase our strongest inclinations, wherever they may lead.

1. Moonlit Madness

I close my eyes to find the deep dark.
I find midnight anywhere.
Peace, the one mammoth moon lights my face aglow
Violent, swirling thoughts now drift and fade
I dream good dreams instead
Desires, nature, and good, good dreams
Make sense to only me
I levitate above morphing kaleidoscopic surfaces
My fingertips are crystallized
Feeling no feelings nor numbness
There is only comforting quiet
I own the terrain and the macrocosm
They see me, bow and serve me as their beloved ruler
Constellations and planets fly by
A symphony of miracles
Circling back to greet me now and again
No earthly frustrations of war or love, for there are
Many many earths here
Numerous as the stars
Revolving around the one big moon, but do not freeze
They make no disturbance
I like it better out here
In the night behind my eyes

Beautiful madness in spatial moonlight
Leave me be.

2. Sandpiper

Sandpiper, cast me to the wind
Don't need no camel to
Cross this here desert
I've got my own feet
Even though my legs are weary
Got just enough water
Even though it trickles out in sweat
These should last me
Until you whisk me
Up and away
Ribbons of sand
Caress my hips
As I
Ascend
Into the warm cerulean air and
The oppressive sun and
The prideful, foolish confidence that
Befell Icarus
The warmth of this sun is no match for you
Sandpiper
Till then, I'll be
Rocking this way and that with
Well-intentioned, gripless footsteps
Toasted sand exfoliating my nose

Eyebrows and upper lip
Eyes admiring the horizon as the
Sun fades, glacially
Below the tops of sand dunes
And the temperature dips
Desert heartbeat
Drum and pat me on

3. Dream Giver

"Give me a dream?"
You ask
But dreams cannot be given.
Inspired, maybe, but
Truly
I cannot give you this
Your dreams must be your own
It is *your* mission alone
To reach inside of yourself
To find the truth of your existence
To decide what you think
To embrace the spaces where your
Soul and consciousness hold court
In the expanse of eternity
To lower your fists and uncurl your fingers
Open your scarred exhausted palms
Hold destiny in *your own* bruised hands
Your dreams must be your beacon
Even if you must travel alone
See, I cannot give you this.
You, alone, are qualified
You must be your own dream giver
As must we all.

4. Little Angry Leaf

Little Angry Leaf
Billows prettily to the ground
Weight of the world
Gusts spin and twirl
It floats and may never come down.

Little Angry Leaf
Turns its bright red face to the Sun
Crimson and cherry
Burgundy Berry
It brawls in wars already won.

Little Angry Leaf
One of many kindred in hue
Closely suspended
Life bitterly ended
For seasons to start anew.

Little Angry Leaf
Gently lands and graces the earth
Lays rest its defense
Surrenders to sequence
Next year's scarlets are proof of its worth.

5. Curiosity

It killed the cat, so they say
But whose cat was it anyway?
Surely not the one who stayed in the house and
Fluffed at yarn and tore pieces of paper for fun
Certainly not the one who clawed at catnip towers and
Battled the sun peaking through the blinds as the sun
ought
Not lions, nor tigers,
Predators of their worlds living in packs and prides
Upper echelon of the food chain
Perhaps, perhaps
The curious cats
Were the indoor pets who ventured out and
Boldly inhaled the scent of fresh cut grass for the first
time
Played with the lush green blades between their paws
Felt the warmth of the sun and a cool tree breeze for the
first time
Without the chilly barrier of a glass window pane
And got stung or bitten by something poisonous
Lurking in the shadows
Burrowing in the dirt
Perhaps, perhaps
The curious cats

Were the big, majestic royalty of the jungle deep
Encountering humans for the first time
And because these big cats were so used to being wild,
Respected predators,
They didn't know that *they* should run
When the people take pictures and pitch tents in the
middle of *their* jungle habitat
Perhaps, perhaps
In the case of the big cat
It was not the big cat's curiosity that caused its demise
Rather, it was humanity's curiosity that
Enabled humanity's recklessness, entitlement, and
Premature self-preservation in a fierce nature that
Humanity should not dare possess
Stray pebbles laying outside of nature and humanity's
established path
Can be so dangerous to
We kitties
Who dare to experience something new
Or merely have newness thrust upon us
So, why do we keep getting warned of
The dangers of curiosity
As if it's all our fault for being curious
When, inevitably,
Naturally, and
By any means,

Curiosity will find us
And have its way?

6. Awakened Hunger

All the lights went out
But now
All of a sudden, I'm awake
I can't see past my hunger, severe thirst
Everything looks fuzzy
Can't feel my cells buzzing anymore,
Not that I noticed before
But the hungrier I get, the stronger I feel
The faster I run
What meal do I crave?
Roasted chicken? No
Shrimp Alfredo? Nah
Steak....hmmmm
Yes, but only if it's rare
But I never liked rare meat before...
I always wanted it medium well...
But the idea of the cool red juice
Dribbling down the sides of a cutting board is quite
Scintillating...
I wonder if I have to cook it at all?
Well that's what they have steak tartare for,
Right?
What's that scent?
Raw steak nearby?

All of a sudden, it feels like a nice day for a run

But I always hated running

I promised myself to only power walk at an incline...

But I guess I'll try running, maybe

Let's just start with a jog

No heavy breathing? No soreness in my throat or lungs?

But it's been 15 minutes straight!

Unbelievable!

I'm not even sweating...

I wonder how fast I can run...

Whoa

That was fast!

Let's go faster

Ugh a fly just flew into my mouth

I think I swallowed a family of gnats

But it was oddly satisfying

Ew, what?!

Oh look: there's a farm!

One, two, five cows, two chickens

And a farmer

That farmer's head is huge!

He must have a big brain...

Delicious... I mean,

Grossss.....right?

Orrrr...Yum?

YUUUUUUMMMMM.

Oh no.

Aw, shit.

Am...

Am I?

Nah, that would be ridiculous....

Ha! Psh, not a chance.

But what ifff...

Am I a vampire?

Can't be, I've been running all night and the sun just came up.

I haven't burst into flames....

What's the thing that's like a vampire but wants flesh too, not just blood?

Werewolf? No

Gremlem? Wait, did that I say right?

Wizard...lizard....zip zip?

Zum zum? No

Zumbum? No, words wrong!

When-words-my-can't-zip-left?!

UGH!!!!

ZombieeeeEEEEE?!?!?!

Zum Zum zum zum zum zummmmmm

Yummmmmmmmmmmmmmmmmmmmmmmmmm

7. The Stuff of Nightmares

Free-falling into a dark abyss
Trying to scream in a burning room but
Your screams,
Though they burn your lungs and strain your throat,
Come out silent and arid as cotton balls
Dancing in the middle of the floor at a party
And when you're done spinning around
It's just you and the dark figure in the corner of the
room
The music slows to a crawling lull
The record player scratches in the groove that
Holds what used to be your favorite part of your favorite
song
You close your eyes
Try to shake and writhe yourself awake
But it's no use
You try to run
But your feet take you nowhere
A toothy grin in the pitch black:
This is the stuff of nightmares.
Thank God they aren't real.
But what about the nightmares that are real?
Based on a lived experience?
The things from which there is no

Running, no
Pinching oneself awake?
What about the lives and the
People living in the present
Who go to sleep to escape the nightmares they live
Only to wake up,
Not relieved
But terrified,
Anguished
All over again
Over and over
No peace awake
No peace asleep.
No rest for the weary.

8. Never, Never

Ignore the seasons
Never, Never
Suppress thy reasons
Never, Never
Sun, monsoons
Weather, Weather

Smoke and whiskey
Leather, Leather
Boot straps, leg slaps
Leather, Leather
Forget thy sailor?
Never, Never

Rope and string
Tethered, Tethered
Kindred puppets
Tethered, Tethered
Free thinking thinkers
Never, Never

You may think it
Clever, Clever
Smoked thought, drunk naught

Mm, Clever, Clever
Ties to reality
Severed, Severed

Strive *and* rest
Endeavor, Endeavor
Love and Laugh
Forever, Ever
Forgive. Forget?
Never, Never
Never. Never.

9. Every Now and Then

Every now and then
Old frustrations
Creep up on me and interrupt my joy
And my sleep
You know what I mean
Old messy situations that I wish ended differently
Overall outcomes I would not change, but
I just wish they ended better
Cleaner
Less casualties
I wonder and worry about the gossip still floating around
about me
Wishing I could show everyone my perspective
Show them that I'm not who the gossips claim me to be
Absolve myself
From the bad things that were and were not my fault
I tell myself the usual:
"What other people think about you is not your business.
As long as you know you did the right thing, it doesn't
matter what anyone else thinks.
Let them talk. That's what they do. All talk.
Endings don't have to be perfect.
You don't have to be perfect, in fact
You're human, and so is everyone else.

None of us will ever be perfect.
Don't lose sleep over it."
But I do
I do lose sleep
And for a moment, or an hour,
I forget myself
I forget all the love I've allowed to occupy my heart
And all the growth I've accomplished since then
I forget that most people are growing, too
And that a good portion of the mutual friends or
acquaintances we share
Can smell the bullshit almost as well as I can
And I forget that the world moves on
Keeps spinning
And that the ecosystem goes on and on
I forget that I'm only one of the many billion people on
Earth
And that everyone has their stories and issues
I forget that maybe no one even gives a shit anymore
And I lose sleep
And I write myself notes at 4am
Because I have to get it out in a space that won't
Regurgitate it back to me
Or make me feel silly for feeling awkward
Frustrated
Anxious
About things that happened

Years and years ago
I have to get it out
In hopes that,
Once the elephant is off my chest
And the imp stops dancing in my brain,
I may resume my sleep
Get good rest
And wake up with my alarm
Feeling entirely different.

10. Celestial Haven

Skating, gliding Saturn's rings,
Your voice echoed my name.
Across the indigo nothingness,
I chased your resonance from star to star.
Complex constellations,
Burning, shooting meteorites
Black holes
Welcomed me, finally, home.
Your orbiting rock,
Your planetary spice and salts
Polished my heel,
Seasoned my blood,
Enveloped me in gravitational bliss.
You pursued my essence,
Shrunk the infinite universe and
Gave it rest inside the stone on my ring finger;
That we may ever choose to ride meteors together
To cosmic coordinates unknown,
When our worlds are too much and not enough.

11. Seasonal Allergies

Nuts, mangoes, shellfish,
Pollen, raw pitted fruits,
Men sometimes,
Flashing lights, high beams, and loud noises.
Is there a vaccine for loud noises?
Is there a needle-free
Allergy therapy
For pitted fruits and madmen?
My body knows when
I've got it in my system
The body knows before the brain does.
And it huffs and it puffs
And implodes.
Zyrtec, Claritin
Benadryl, EpiPen
Fresh air when it's cold outside
Sunshine on the face when it's warm
Good friends and close family
These are the only remedies that exist
In my existence thus far
Other than that,
I'm wingin' it.

12. The Exact Same Rain

The exact same rain that
Once brought me peace and comfort
Now makes me uncomfortable
I used to love how the world would slow down
How the water washed all the debris from the air
Knowing the trees and the flowers would have what they
needed to flourish.
Raindrops making love music on tin roofs and
Lush, swaying palm leaves were
Hypnotic, seductive.
Raindrops sliding rhythmically down window panes, the
Thunder rumbling the earth and your base, were
Just enough to make you want to
Dial that number saved in your phone as
"DO NOT CALL"
Or "IDIOT"
But diagonal raindrops in the distance?
Raindrops I can't hear or feel?
Those make me sad these days.
The landscape isn't enough anymore.
Something to do with the limited space
Never enough windows or
Steamy beverages these days
Scarcely enough sunlight

Then again, there never was.
What changed?

13. Someday

Someday, I suspect
It'll all be a little easier
I won't hold my breath before crowds
I won't suck in my stomach
I'll fight without hesitation or regret
I will forget the taste of fear
Someday you won't recognize me.

14. Villain's Origin

Gettin' real sick of
Gettin' short ends of these sticks
Chippin' away at these here boulders
By myself
Clawin' at the grime for the greater good
Knowin' the greater good wouldn't
Give a rusty penny for me
You tellin' me I'm not it
You actin' like I'm not everything
When we both know I am
Like I'm not right
Just 'cause you don't want to be wrong
Just 'cause you don't want to learn
Well, I got news for you
Just 'cause your world is too small
Don't mean I'm too big
Your lil' world
Is a fruit gnat buzzin' 'round my
Sweet, sweet backside.
Maybe you should kiss it.

15. Spice Symphony

Sage, Cinnamon, Thyme
Basil, Cardamom, Ginger
Vanilla Bean, Clove

16. Expiration Dates

You let the tea sit in your mug for too long
Yes, I know it was healthy before
Yes, I know the expiration date wasn't written on the box
But you let it sit too long
You left it, undisturbed, for days and weeks
And now, what would have offered you healing
properties
Is slimy gook
And thick sediment
A tawny stain circling the porcelain rim
If you sip it now, you will be sick
Dump it
Wash your mug
Try again
Drink it while it's still hot
I hope that wasn't your last tea bag

17. Unhinged

I'm off my hinge
I don't open and close like I'm meant to
I don't swing smoothly
My rough edges abrade violently against the frame
My brass handles have faded indents where
Countless thumbs and forefingers pulled me
To and fro
I could use a sandpaper polish
A fresh coat of paint
A little grease and that missing screw
Till then
I'll be hanging here
Watching you come and go
Moving when you will me so
Until you stop and
Pay enough attention to
Realize
I don't move like I used to
Show me a little TLC

18. Before You Get Married

Before you get married,
And soon after your engagement,
If you haven't already,
Go to therapy for yourself as an individual
And get premarital counseling together from a licensed
therapist.
Go routinely.
There is no shame in going once a month, or once a
week, or multiple times a week.
Let it ebb and flow as you need.
And at least plan quarterly check-ins for the 1st year of
your marriage
(Or monthly if you find yourself having to make multiple
big life decisions at the same time)
There's a whole lot of adjustment going on
Even after you say "I do"
You don't want to brush it off
You don't want to bury it or ignore it
You don't want to miss it.
While you're planning the wedding,
Regardless of how extravagant or how intimate,
You will experience myriad emotions
You may hit a point where you
Question everything, including each other

You may not be able to see the sky or the sun or the
forest through the trees
Therapy and premarital counseling will walk you
through all that
It will equip you with tools for success
I don't care if it sounds corny
It can save your marriage a million times over
And heal pieces of you both that you didn't even know
were broken
Even after 8 years or any long time of knowing each
other
It will help you make sense of your emotions
It will help you both break down the fights and the walls
Get to the root of the issues
And realize that you are not each other's opponents
It will help you find solutions together
And create healthy patterns for conflict resolution
And realistic expectations for yourself and others
It will help you define the partnership you want and
need in your life
It will help you deal with family members and
Wedding planners
And bridal parties
And invoices
And money
And panic
And cold feet

And bad dreams
And your relationship with food
And making the thousand decisions you will have to
make during this time frame
It will help you stay in touch with
Who YOU are and
Who YOU want to be
So that you don't lose yourself in this
Criminally underestimated process
But for any of it to work
You have to approach it humbly with the goal of
resolution and progress
There will be finger pointing and
There will be accountability
You may have to burn it down to build it back up
You may have to start from scratch
You will need to let go of the need to be right
And fully embrace that you three are having the
conversation to strengthen and
Improve your love and partnership
From root to branch to leaf,
Down to the ground and the sap and the wind,
Wherever your leaves may overflow and scatter.
You really have to prepare yourselves to be just you two
and God
(And a really good licensed therapist when needed)
Against the entire world

And be satisfied with that if that's all it will ever be
You have to be willing to accept the hard truths
And be okay with no one understanding except you two
You have to be ready to shed your responsibilities to
everyone and everything else and
Take first responsibility for each other and yourselves
Marriage is the big heavy, but
It. Is. Possible.
It. Is. Attainable.
It can be so. Much. Fun.
You just have to put in the work to reap the benefits.
Just like farming
Keeping pets and house plants alive
Studying for tests
Getting that promotion
And most other things in life.
It really can be done well.

19. When

33

When the world breaks
When the sky falls
When our sun, moon, and stars
Plunge into the sea
When there is no more breath
Nor air
No chocolate sundaes
Or sunsets
I'll rest peacefully
Knowing we loved each other well

20. Embracing the Twilight Studio

I've had to accept that God chooses
Late nights and early mornings
To do His best work in me
To invoke a level of openness
Expression
Nakedness
That I often struggle to access in daylight
I would find myself agitated when awakened from my
dreams
Or lack thereof
(You know, the deep peaceful darkness)
I would pray and pray to God
To quiet my overwhelming feelings
To halt my haunting thoughts
So I could get rest to prepare for the things
I would undoubtedly face when
The sun came up
But God said,
"Not so."
In the wee hours, it appears
I have work to do
Once it became a pattern
I decided to stop getting mad and

Just let it all flow
To my delicious surprise, I found that,
Although I may lose an hour or two of sleep,
The creative offloading truly is
Rest
For me
And, most times, I do get back to sleep afterward
And I wake up feeling more refreshed than I would
Had I tried to force myself to
Sleep through it
And who would want to miss this?
Allllll this?
I get a front row seat to witness my
Most flawed, complex, strange and splendid
Soul fragments
Forged into art.
And so, I've accepted
That my soul's work
Will be done in the twilight studio
While most people on this side of the world are asleep
It's okay
And I'm okay with it
It makes me okay
And it makes me better.

21. Morning Coffee

More than most scents,
I enjoy the smell of piping hot morning coffee with
Caramel Macchiato creamer and
How the steam rises and swirls above the rim
Letting the plants and my brain know that I am
Safe
Early in the morning
I love living up in the sky, and that
When I look through my wall
Of big windows that lead to the balcony,
All I see is a forest of trees
The trees and I, we awaken together
I love how softly,
How gently the sun rises to
Greet new possibilities, and
The push-pin freckled walls behind my desk and
All around this open room
Bloom
From indigo, to violet, to magenta,
Tangerine, and then warm,
Sunflower Gold
When the raw brilliance of
Nature's chroma
Magnifies the snug silence

I am shrouded in love, and
I am at peace with
Whatever woke me up
In the witching hours.